Writer's Toolkit & Workbook

Over 150 Free Apps,
Tips & Tricks
by

Abbey Johns

About the Author

I am a writer and write fiction and non fiction. I like to mix it up – sometimes a blog, maybe an article, a video or Slide Share (www.slideshare.net). I like gadgets and technology. I like to practice using new techniques and am addicted. Technically I believe I am called an early adopter. There are just not enough hours in the day.

So I started collecting my apps and programmes and put them all in a workbook for me to keep close at all times. And here it is. A workbook and toolkit for writers and authors.

I call it my Appy Book, because if I don't have it, I am Un'appy!

If you have any comments or want to suggest an app, I would love to hear from you.

Please drop me a line at abbey.johns@ponder-yonder.com.

Writing is a form of therapy;
sometimes I wonder how
all those who do not write, compose or paint can
manage to escape the madness, melancholia, the
panic and fear which is inherent
in a human situation.

Graham Greene

Introduction

Thank you for buying this Writer's Toolkit and Workbook in a jungle of other books about shortcuts and hacks.

The tools listed here are as useful to an author with 20 books, as they are to a complete beginner, starting out on the adventure. This workbook has the potential to increase productivity and quality of anyone's writing.

At the last count, there were over one hundred and thirty-five resources for you to check out and over 120 of these are free. I tried them all, as part of my research for this workbook.

The idea for this book started when I could not find information saved for my latest book project. I knew I stored it somewhere and searched all over, even my social media accounts. I did not find what I needed, so in frustration, I took a rest break for a couple of hours. Another wasted session. I realised this happened a lot!

This workbook and toolkit will help all those who spend more time looking for saved information than writing. Or those who have searched for and downloaded the same PDF twice from a website? Or horrors, updated a blog or story only to find you've updated the wrong version? That definitely takes some beating for writers in a hurry.

Do you have loads of different places for keeping writing tools or research? I use Scrivener, Cloud storage, paper and electronic notebooks, my PC and voice memos.

Perhaps, like me, you're an experimenter and try apps from 'Apps Gone Free' (apple.co/1YIRphV)? Or Appsumo Deals (bit.ly/1YISwhA); or browse the top free and paid apps online?

Mostly, I store my work in Dropbox, but I have used iCloud and Onedrive, which I pay for, so I need to use them. Right?

And, I have stuff in Evernote and Pocket too. Meaning, I read some dazzling pieces, and then never find them again. If you resonate with this - then this workbook is for you.

This Workbook and Toolkit

Writers need something to keep by their side for startling insights you don't want to lose. So as well as an aide memoir for everything creative, this workbook becomes your journal too. There is plenty of white space to jot down notes. Yes, I have a real live, honest to goodness, purpose built, workbook here for you to take everywhere.Put a sticker on your front door as a reminder - keys, purse, wallet, glasses, phone, and charger. AND this workbook. Never leave home without it.

Writing

Let's not kid ourselves - writing a book, blog or updating your website takes time and effort. Not just once a week but, to be successful, about four times a week.

You need to lay your hands on what you want – fast. You need to write quickly. But you need quality in your writing too. This workbook and toolkit provide both commodities: a written reminder of what you use each app for and filters and programmes to improve the written word.I do not have any affiliations to the tools listed here; my recommendations are from experience.

How to Use This Book

Here are my best tips, hacks, apps, videos. About 130, although I keep adding to them as I find another. The majority are free. As a bonus, I've included a short list of my essential paid apps or tools I couldn't do without as a writer.

The book is in chronological book-writing order. Giving you a clue of where to find tools and help, depending on where you are in writing. Sections include Images, Work Quicker, Writing Training Programmes, and so on. Within each chapter is an alphabetical list of apps, programmes or videos.

There is also a complete alphabetical list of the apps, downloads, etc., at the end of the book. Print this and stick it on your writer's noticeboard for easy access.

The updated list will be on my website too: www.ponder-yonder.com for you to download.

You will need to register though – you guessed that right?

I have left space in the workbook for you to record how you got on with an app. Issues such as:

- **How the app/programme worked**
- **If it was a free trial and when that expires**
- **How and where you used it (e.g., fiction, nonfiction, image, book, plugin)**
- **Where it stored (e.g., desktop, folder, extension, programme files, download**

For some of the apps, you will see a check mark or tick in their box – which shows I think it quite brilliant.

I have added brief notes on how simple a programme or hack is to use, and other relevant, important points as I see it.

Short Codes

I have used shortcodes to help with downloads. Some long links would stretch across two typed lines if I included the full hyperlink. To keep the text pretty, you will see shortcodes in the text (just like LOL for 'laugh out loud' or OMG for 'Oh my God').

For example the shortcode for my website www.http://Ponder-Yonder.com. is: bit.ly/1Tzhyys , copy the shortcode into your browser and press enter, and my site appears. Shortcodes save you time and effort.

Now let's get going...

Table of Contents

	Chapter	
1.	Research on Your Book or Blog	1
2.	Creative	7
3.	Images	13
4.	Writing	23
5.	No Distractions	35
6.	Language	41
7.	Quality of Writing	47
8.	Your Website or Blog	51
9.	Design	57
10.	Video	63
11.	Social Media	67
12.	Work Quicker	73
13.	Storage	79
14.	Writing Training Programmes	85
15.	Sales and Marketing	91
16.	Communications	97
17.	Gems and General	103
18.	Bonus – My Top Paid Apps	113
19.	Before You Go	119
20.	*Glossary*	
21.	*Alphabetical List of Resources*	
22.	*Notes Pages*	

1. Research

Collect and find information on the web
using many different hacks and apps.
Here are my free favourites

Alltop: http://alltop.com/

Use Alltop for top news headlines from around the web.
Create your own 'My Alltop' and a "personal, online magazine rack" of your favourite websites and blogs. Choose from a collection of over 32,000 information sources—if you're interested in something, they probably have it covered.

Easy to use and set up for the beginner.

Feedly: https://feedly.com/

Organise, read and share web information that matters to you. Set up RSS (really simple syndication) feeds into your inbox to save you time visiting individual sites.

Difficult to set up in your own inbox – but worth the effort

My Notes

Date Accessed
Where is it now?
Used For?
Comments

Google Alerts: https://www.google.com/alerts

I have been using Google alerts for three years now. It's a content change detection and notification service.The service sends emails to you when it finds new results— web pages, newspaper articles, blogs, or scientific research—for subjects you've chosen.

Upload directly into social media channels or save for future use in your book or blog

Google Earth: https://earth.google.com/

Google Earth allows you a view of the earth via satellite imagery, maps, terrain, and 3D views of buildings. You can look at galaxies in outer space or canyons in the ocean.

You can use the programme to research street scenes or exotic locations for books, plays or film.

Try the street view for real detail

My Notes

Date Accessed
Where is it now?
Used For?
Comments

Quora: http://en.wikipedia.org/wiki/Quora

Quora is a question-and-answer website where people ask
sometimes odd or risky questions, like:

- **What's it like to have someone die in your arms?**
- **What is the loveliest thing a child has ever said to you?**
- **How much does a YouTuber with a million subscribers make in a year?**

Use Quora to research a book, blog or article topic.
Careful, you could lose a couple of hours in these pages.

Title Generator: http://www.noemata.net/pa/titlegen/

The title generator gives totally random word
combinations for artworks, books, and fictional
character names.
Here are my first three random titles for a new blog:

1. **Underlined Plan of Death**
2. **My Falling Substance**
3. **The Sentiment of Sorrow**

My Notes

Date Accessed
Where is it now?
Used For?
Comments

Wikipedia: https://www.wikipedia.org/

The free online encyclopedia.

World Building: http://worldbuilding.stackexchange.com/

A question and answer site for writers/artists, using science, geography, and culture to construct imaginary worlds and settings.

No site registration required.

My Notes

Date Accessed
Where is it now?
Used For?
Comments

2. Creative

Where and how to start your book?
Or what can you blog about?
Then what structure will the story
or article have?
Try these apps if you are stuck.

Curator: http://curator.co

Organise your thoughts visually, refine your visual storytelling, collect inspiration, create mood boards and export them to PDF or share them directly or collaborate on visual reference library.
There is a free version, upgrade for more options

Infogr.am: https://infogr.am/

Create infographics and interactive online charts.
Super easy with great tutorials.

My Notes

Date Accessed
Where is it now?
Used For?
Comments

Simple Mind Maps:
http://www.simpleapps.eu/simplemind

Designed to synchronise
your Mind Maps across
platforms. Available
for most systems.

I like the way you can
manipulate the nodes on
the iPad with your finger
for this programme.

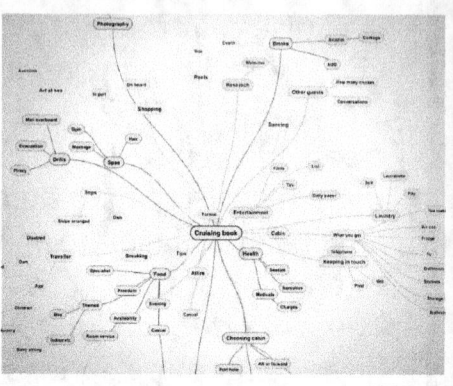

Soovle: http://www.soovle.com/

Soovle is a search engine of search engines. Useful for
two main purposes. Firstly, if you've a vague idea
what you're looking for but don't know exactly.
 Secondly, it's great for keyword research and ideas.
You can see suggestions pulled from all sorts of search
engines, including niche ones.

You can also save your searches to use later. Great app

My Notes

Date Accessed
Where is it now?
Used For?
Comments

Storystarter: http://www.thestorystarter.com/

Story Starter randomly generates
215,572,250,880 story starters.
Use this idea generator for short
stories, novels, plays, movie
scripts, or just for fun.
It might help with writers block.

Xmind Map: http://www.xmind.net/

XMind is excellent mind mapping and brainstorming
software, serving more than a million users around
the world.

Their purpose (quoted on website) is to develop the
best productivity tool, save people's time and raise
the efficiency of writers.

My Notes

Date Accessed
Where is it now?
Used For?
Comments

3. Images

I am no graphic artist and it has taken me hours to figure out how to insert images into different formats and styles. I'm still learning.

Save yourself some time and try these apps and information sources for a head start.

3D Book Cover: Bit.ly/1RtsMjt (Video)

Watch this You Tube video for a
simple and effective way of creating
a 3D image of your book cover

Canva: https://www.canva.com/

Design your own book covers
and images.
A brilliant way to create any design
with templates and intuitive drag
and drop features. Upload your
photographs. Or make a post on
twitter.
I made this book and book cover o
 Canva - see an early draft here.

Writers Toolkit and Workbook
Includes
Over 135
ree.Apps/Hacks

ABBEY JOHNS

My Notes

Date Accessed
Where is it now?
Used For?
Comments

Flickr: https://www.flickr.com/

Store your camera roll or your photo's free and have access to others for unique images. You only need to register if uploading content onto the website

For mobile users, Flickr has official mobile apps for iOS, Android, and PlayStation Vita, operating systems, and an optimised mobile website.

The first upload of images may be complicated.

Freepik: http://www.freepik.com/about

The leading site for free vector designs (so they claim). Some lovely images here.

My Notes

Date Accessed
Where is it now?
Used For?
Comments

Gimp: https://www.gimp.org/

GIMP is an acronym for GNU Image Manipulation Program; a freely distributed program for photo retouching, image composition and image authoring. The terms of usage and rules about copying are listed in the GNU General Public License. A free alternative to Photoshop.

Watch a YouTube video on how to create layers here: *https://youtu.be/8LmW5ndnEqw*

Google Images: https://images.google.com/

A search service owned by Google, allowing users to search the Web for image content.The keywords for the image search are based on the filename of the image, the link text pointing to the image, and text adjacent to the image.
When the user clicks on an image it is displayed in its original website. The user can then close the box and browse the website, or view the full-sized image itself.

My Notes

Date Accessed
Where is it now?
Used For?
Comments

Instant Eyedropper:
http://instant-eyedropper.com/

A free colour detection tool for image and web builders. Identifies and automatically pastes to the clipboard the HTML colour code of any pixel on the screen with just a single mouse click.

It's a great tool for matching colours and for branding.

Jing: http://jing.en.softonic.com/

Jing is a simple to use screen capture tool; a yellow sun sits on the edge of your PC ready for action all the time.
Chose a part of the computer screen that you want to make a picture of, highlite, save and copy. Ta da!
You can also make 5-minute videos for marketing your books and upload to YouTube

My favourite free, cut and paste image tool

My Notes

Date Accessed
Where is it now?
Used For?
Comments

Pablo: https://pablo.buffer.com/app

You can create beautiful images easily to make your posts pop. Use directly into your social media posts. Here's one I made earlier

Pic2pixlr: Bit.ly/1ThAmzQ

Another Chrome extension used for changing images in the Pixlr image factory.

Free photo enhancing and editing software also included. For beginners and seasoned pros.

My Notes

Date Accessed
Where is it now?
Used For?
Comments

Pixabay: https://pixabay.com/

All images and videos on Pixabay are released free of copyrights under Creative Commons.

You may download, modify, distribute, and use them royalty free for anything you like, even in commercial applications. Attribution is not required., which means they are free for copy write purposes

Sizes of Images (Infographic):Bit.ly/1rQUtxV

All the sizes of each image for social media display. A well-used cheat sheet for me.

From Hubspot.

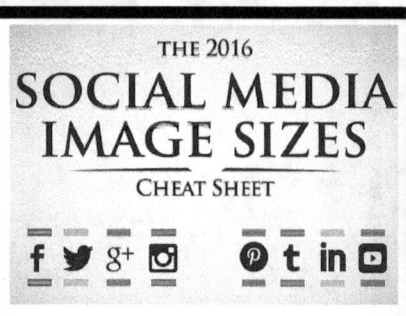

My Notes

Date Accessed
Where is it now?
Used For?
Comments

Unsplash: https://unsplash.com/

Beautiful hi-definition and unusual free images

Wordle: http://www.wordle.net

Put your most used phrases and words in a word cloud to display to make a display on your website. Choose from loads of fonts and layouts.

Here's my first attempt.

My Notes

Date Accessed
Where is it now?
Used For?
Comments

WP Clip Art: http://www.wpclipart.com/index.html

Over 68K
public domain images

Here's an example

My Favourites

Details:

My Notes

Date Accessed
Where is it now?
Used For?
Comments

4. Writing

This is the heart of the writer's skill and therefore a large section in this toolkit. Choose which programme you need by experimenting with all of these.

Apple Pages: http://www.apple.com/ios/pages/

Apple's word processing tool

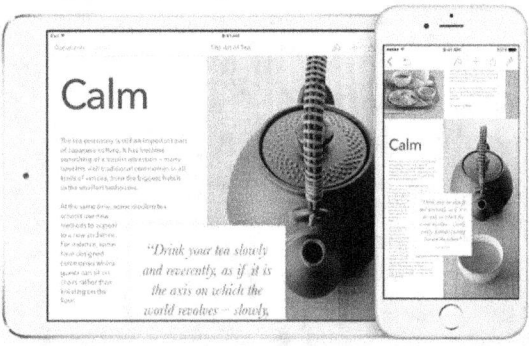

Blurb Booksmart: http://www.blurb.com/make/booksmart

Blurb is more a self-publishing tool, but a simple way to design the layout of your work and see what it looks like if published.

You don't have to pay anything to use the software.

My Notes

Date Accessed
Where is it now?
Used For?
Comments

Create Space: https://www.createspace.com/

Print on demand and
eBook creator with loads
of free tools to make the
publishing easy. Also
includes distribution and
marketing services, plus
you can chose paid
support services such
editing.

Easy Book: http://easybook-project.org/

E-Book reading software providing a 'paperback'
experience on the computer screen: The pages turn
when you click them, just like a real book.

Also, select a textured background to make the
pages seem like real paper.

My Notes

Date Accessed
Where is it now?
Used For?
Comments

Editorial Calendars (1): http://bit.ly/1PAqEHk

This post by David Moth of E-Consultancy lists some free calendars to personlise and use:

Vertical Measures: http://bit.ly/1PAsGHk
Postcron: http://bit.ly/1PArpAi
Hubspot: http://bit.ly/1PArUKr
Lightbox Collaborative: http://bit.ly/1PAsoSn
Wordpress plug in: http://bit.ly/1PArUKy
Web.Search.Social: http://bit.ly/1PAsqbj
Bob Angus: http://bit.ly/1PAsbNx

Editorial Calendars (2): http://bit.ly/1PAssjw

I use the Content Marketing Strategy Calendar and adapted it to suit me. A google email account is required. Keep it on your desktop or Dropbox

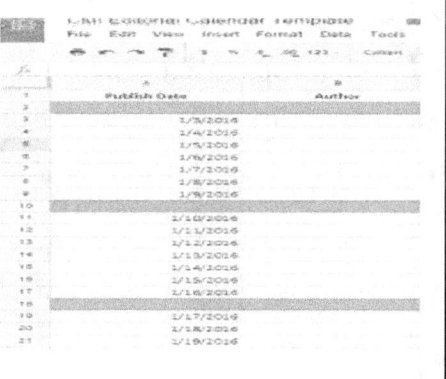

My Notes

Date Accessed
Where is it now?
Used For?
Comments

Gingko: https://gingkoapp.com/

> Gingko is a new kind of tool; that lets you share your ideas with lists, outlines and cards, all in the same clean interface. Let your thoughts flow freely into place.
>
> Watch a video on YouTube:
> *https://youtu.be/egCKZHsICm8*

Google Docs: https://www.google.com/docs/about/

> Get yourself a Google account and use the storage to keep all your files you save. Available offline too.
>
> My absolute favourite for non-fiction book writing and research. This programme inserts links directly into text passages. Superb.

My Notes

> Date Accessed
> Where is it now?
> Used For?
> Comments

iBooks Author: http://apple.co/1TRcJ3K

Just like Kindle except it is for Apple and IOS systems

Get started with the iBooks Author Starter Kit — a step-by-step guide, plus all of the multi-media materials you need to get started.

Learn more about using iBooks Author, or download it from the Mac App Store for free and start creating Multi-Touch learning materials.

Index Cards: http://bit.ly/1TRzK6p

This is a corkboard writing app for iPad or iPhone that makes it easy to capture, organise, and collect ideas. Whether you're an author, screenwriter or researcher, Index Card can help you become more efficient and organised.

See a video about it here:
https://youtu.be/Q8_mSmA3tTI

My Notes

Date Accessed
Where is it now?
Used For?
Comments

Kindle Scout: https://kindlescout.amazon.com/

Kindle Scout is reader-powered publishing for new, never-before-published books. It's a place where readers help decide if a book gets published.

Kindle Press then publish selected books.
You receive 5-year renewable terms, a $1,500 advance, 50% eBook royalty rate, easy rights reversions and featured Amazon marketing.

Microsoft Word: https://office.live.com/start/Word.aspx

The online free version.
Save documents in One Drive and share with others too. My absolute favourite for Kindle conversion.

I could not live as an author without Microsoft Word.

My Notes

Date Accessed
Where is it now?
Used For?
Comments

One Page Novel Spreadsheet: Bit.ly/1qyBFCq

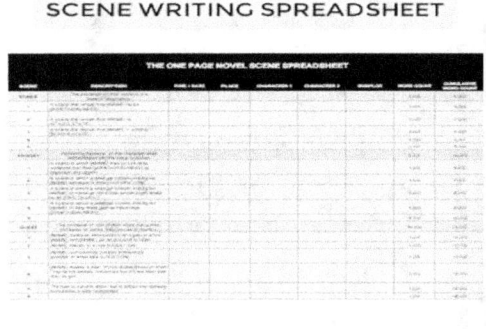

An 8-stage plot formula
creating strong
character development.
Instructions for use are
included in the
download (you have to
use Google Docs); all
the word count updates
at once. Clever.

Sigil: https://sigil-ebook.com/about

An amazing open source programme that lets you
create industry standard formats from a word
document. Do not try this if you are new to coding but
if you want to have a go watch this video training from
Rob Cubbon: *https://youtu.be/A_Z8aQeEMmg*

Fantastic resource but takes time to learn.

Download available from *http://sigil.en.softonic.com/*

My Notes

Date Accessed
Where is it now?
Used For?
Comments

Storybook: http://www.novelist.ch/joomla/

There are charts and different ways of laying out your project if you like visual aids/presentations.

You can store complete information about characters and locations in one place. Then, use the included Storybook features for managing chapters, scenes, characters and locations, items and tags.

Writing for Kindle: https://kdp.amazon.com/

Self-publishing
platform for eBooks

My Notes

Date Accessed
Where is it now?
Used For?
Comments

yWriter: http://www.spacejock.com/yWriter5.html

YWriter breaks your novel into chapters and scenes, helping track your work while leaving your mind free to create. Designed by an author for authors.

Although yWriter is for novels, enterprising users have created their own translation files to customise the program for plays, non-fiction, and even sermons.

Other tools available on this site - great resource.

My Favourites

Details:

My Notes

Date Accessed
Where is it now?
Used For?
Comments

5. No Distractions

All writers have a preferred place of writing whether in peace and quiet or with music blaring through the headphones.
When you are feeling less than motivated, though, it's easy to play online games or read the news. These next apps and programmes will help you focus.

Cold Turkey: http://getcoldturkey.com/

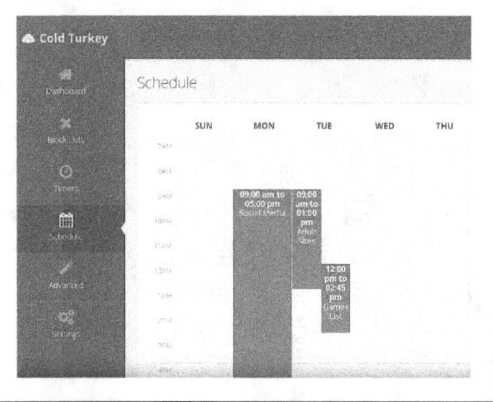

A Windows programme. It temporarily blocks distracting websites.

FocusWriter: http://gottcode.org/focuswriter/

Don't let the black screen with the green font in the video scare you off; you can set up different themes and colours.

FocusWriter is a simple, distraction-free writing environment.

My Notes

Date Accessed
Where is it now?
Used For?
Comments

Noisli: http://www.noisli.com/

Plug into this little app to block out outside noise, or mimic a coffee shop or train journey.

Or even combine a rainstorm and a dark night. Whatever gets you writing.

Pomodoro Technique: Bit.ly/1TRBpcb

Divide your projects up into 25-minute chunks and earn breaks as you go along.

Try it here using the timer on the website.

My Notes

Date Accessed
Where is it now?
Used For?
Comments

Self Control: http://selfcontrolapp.com/

For the Mac only

SelfControl

A free Mac application to help you avoid distracting websites.

Write or Die: http://writeordie.com/

For PC or try the newer mobile version.
Write or Die claims to put the "prod" in productivity
by using negative reinforcement. There are
three modes:
- **Gentle Mode: Nice reminders to continue writing**
- **Normal Mode: Nasty sounds if you disobey gentle mode**
- **Kamikaze Mode: Keep writing or your work unwrites itself!!**

Scary when your writing starts disappearing!

My Notes

Date Accessed
Where is it now?
Used For?
Comments

6. Language

The detail that gives a writer their voice is the language used. Here are some useful apps and websites that enrich your vocabulary.

Neatorama: Bit.ly/1qyz1N7

Gives the origins of
familiar phrases here, like
"steal someone's
thunder" or "paying
through the nose", and an
absorbing website too.

Thesaurus: http://www.thesaurus.com/

This app functions as a phone and tablet app.
Designed for on-the-go access to a comprehensive
phrase thesaurus.

Look up a keyword or phrase and see related literary
phrases, which can help you come up with a more
creative phrase of your own

My Notes

Date Accessed
Where is it now?
Used For?
Comments

Types of Literary Terms: Bit.ly/1qyzjDC

A beautiful reference site. Includes easily understood terms such as narrative and tropes, plus sets out the types of genres for your books.

You can lose a lot of time, just following the links, on this site.

WordLists: Bit.ly/1qyArqR

A collection of different types of word lists & synonyms

An **idiom** is a phrase that means what it means, even if it doesn't make sense.

"You can't teach an old dog new tricks."

My Notes

Date Accessed
Where is it now?
Used For?
Comments

Word Web: http://wordweb.info/free/

Toss out that dog-eared dictionary and worn-out
thesaurus, and use this helpful tool instead.
Word web has:

- **One-click access in almost any Windows program**
- **Hundreds of thousands of definitions and synonyms**
- **Updated with the latest international English words**
- **Works offline, or reference to Wikipedia and
  web references**

My Favourites:

Details:

My Notes

Date Accessed
Where is it now?
Used For?
Comments

7. Quality of Writing

Watch out for the mechanics of writing. Where do the apostrophe's go and should it be choose or chose? Mistakes in grammar or choice of word can be distracting and bring readers out of your fictional world.

Try these sources to help.

Blog Topic Generator: http://bit.ly/1TRsVBV

Add three nouns to get a week's worth of blog titles
constructed for you. I added three nouns, 'writer',
'productive', 'tips and tricks'=

- **15 Best Blogs to Follow About Writers**
- **10 Quick Tips about Tip and Tricks**
- **How to Solve the biggest Problem with Productivity**
- **Why We Love Writers (and You Should , Too)**
- **10 Myths about Tips and Tricks**

Its a start anyway!

Grammarly: https://www.grammarly.com

So much better than a spell checker – when added to
Chrome as an extension. It also gives suggestions for
a richer vocabulary and highlights plagiarised text

 grammarly

My Notes

Date Accessed
Where is it now?
Used For?
Comments

ProWritingAid: https://prowritingaid.com/

Free manuscript editing software. Check your own writing for overused words, vague abstract and complex words as well as spelling and grammar.

Go premium for more features.

Wordcounter: http://www.wordcounter.com/

Are there some words you use too much? How many times have you written 'splendid' or 'laughing' in a document?

Paste your work in here and this clever programme lets you know.

My Notes

Date Accessed
Where is it now?
Used For?
Comments

8. Your Website Or Blog

Have you got your own website or thinking of building one?

This chapter has some great assets to help

Blogger: http/www.blogger.com/

Free weblog publishing tool from Google, for sharing text, photos and video.

Free templates/themes and gadgets.

Coffee Cup Editor: Bit.ly1Z8LXoK

Learn how to tweak your own web pages using HTML (the language of the web). Difficult though.

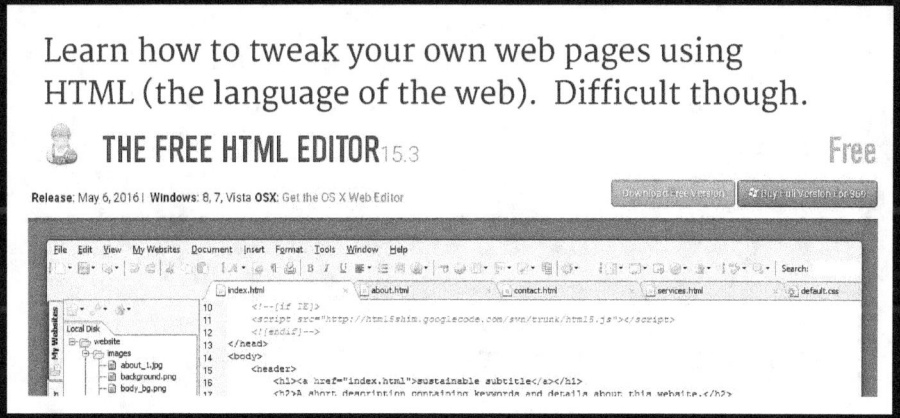

My Notes

Date Accessed
Where is it now?
Used For?
Comments

Favicon: http://www.favicon.cc/

Ever wondered how
the tabs in your
browser have a tiny
little icon logo? Go to
Favicon and make one
for your website

Favicons (favorite icons) are the small images that are
associated with a website. They will be displayed on the
address bar, on browser tabs, and in the bookmark list.

Google Analytics: https://analytics.google.com/

Google Analytics is a freemium web analytics service
offered by Google that tracks and reports website
traffic.

Use to find how many visitors to your website and
which pages they spend the most time on.

Difficult to set up all but the basic programmes.

My Notes

Date Accessed
Where is it now?
Used For?
Comments

PressThis: Bit.ly/1Z8KM8X

If you use Wordpress to run your website, use this mumbo-jumbo or coding as it's called, to copy text/video/images straight into a blog post.

Watch a video and see how to do it.
https://youtu.be/yHFUUOZxQXg

Recite This: http://www.recitethis.com/

Add your quote and Recite offers options for display - here's one I did earlier.

WRITE RIGHT, RIGHT?

My Notes

Date Accessed
Where is it now?
Used For?
Comments

WordPress: https://wordpress.com/

A programme that lets you start your website (my website runs on WordPress). One of my top writing tools.

To set up your website watch this video from YouTube: *https://youtu.be/8Jv47_VIBOQ*

I used this video resource for my website. Great for detail and explanation. Funny too.

My Favourites:

Details:

My Notes

Date Accessed
Where is it now?
Used For?
Comments

9. Design

Designing the formatting of a book
or your website?
Try these useful apps and programmes

CoverCritics: http://covercritics.com/

Upload your book cover and get some feedback from the web community

See comments on my original cover for this book at: *http://covercritics.com/?p=1537*

It's not pretty, but useful feedback

Does My Cover Suck: Bit.ly/1Z8NpaJ

Is your book cover hot or not? Have you the courage to upload your newly designed eBook cover?

Looks good fun.

My Notes

Date Accessed
Where is it now?
Used For?
Comments

Doodle: http://doodle.com/

A great scheduling
tool mostly used for
meetings when lots
of people involved.
Link to Evernote
and conduct free
polls of book covers
and A/B testing.

17 June 2016					
	9:00	11:00	2:00	4:00	8:00
Tom		✓		✓	
Paula	✓	✓	✓		✓
Chris		✓		✓	✓
	☐	☐	☐	☐	☐

FontFaceNinja: http://www.fontface.ninja/

You're broswing a website and you want to find the
name of a font? Here comes the ninja!

Add this app to your browser and discover what font
each website is using just by clicking on one word.

My Notes

Date Accessed
Where is it now?
Used For?
Comments

Free Fonts – Five websites to try:

- **1001 Free Fonts:**
  http://www.1001freefonts.com
- **DaFont: http://www.dafont.com/**
- **FontPark: http://www.fontpark.net/en/**
- **Google Fonts:**
  https://www.google.com/fonts
- **Beautiful Web Type:**
  http://hellohappy.org/beautiful-web-type

TypeGenius: http://www.typegenius.com/

Find the perfect font combo
for your next book or blog
project . Chose one font and
TypeGenius gives you some
well researched options to
complement your choice

My Notes

Date Accessed
Where is it now?
Used For?
Comments

10. Video

If a picture paints a thousand words then a video's word count goes off the scale .
Something writers always appreciate

Adobe Spark: https://standout.adobe.com/voice

A free iOS app lets you make an impact with an amazing animated video.

Persuade, inform and inspire anyone on-line.

Easy to use and produce.

Animoto: https://animoto.com

Free video making software, provides templates for inserting music and images.

See one I made earlier for my EBook:

"Cruising Holidays Decoded"
https://youtu.be/EWvn126PyZE

My Notes

Date Accessed
Where is it now?
Used For?
Comments

Youtube: https://www.youtube.com

> Upload or make your videos here. Use for self-promotion or marketing your books. Create your own channel for tempting subscribers.
>
> Here is one I made earlier for my book on cruising – I used Animoto to make the video and YouTube to display.
>
> *https://youtu.be/EWvn126PyZE*

Powtoon: https://www.powtoon.com

> Allows someone with no technical or design skills to create engaging professional "look and feel" animated presentations.
>
> See Powtoons video explanation here:
> *https://www.powtoon.com/index/*

My Notes

> Date Accessed
> Where is it now?
> Used For?
> Comments

11. Social Media

Where would we be without the social media pages to promote our books and blogs? Here are those I use regularly but there are more.
See useful article here - How Successful Authors Use Social Media to Sell Their Books:*http://bit.ly/1tg9Cte*

Bitley: https://bitly.com

> Fed up with having long clickable links?
> My cruising book link is soooo long:
>
> *https://www.amazon.co.uk/Cruising-Holidays-Decoded-Tips-Tricks-ebook/dp/B014VL4E0U?ie=UTF8&*Version*=1&*entries*=0*
>
> Use a bitlink where it becomes a short and easier to type – *http://amzn.to/1SHG3Jq*

Buffer: https://buffer.com/

> Use the buffer extension and app to schedule all your social media tweets for holidays or to get ahead of yourself.
>
> Choose how many times a day you want to tweet. Also, select feeds from your favourite websites to pick up great content for tweets too.

My Notes

> Date Accessed
> Where is it now?
> Used For?
> Comments

Facebook: https://www.facebook.com

Not just for friends and family. Start your own business page and promote your books.

Have a look at JKRowlings page:
https://www.facebook.com/JKRowling/?fref=ts

Or Stephen King:
https://www.facebook.com/OfficialStephenKing/

Hootsuite: https://hootsuite.com

With the ability to manage all your social networks and schedule messages for future publishing,

Hootsuite gives you a range of options for your social media activity

My Notes

Date Accessed
Where is it now?
Used For?
Comments

Pinterest: https://www.pinterest.com

Put 'Authors' or 'Writers' in the search box and find thousands of interesting boards and references.

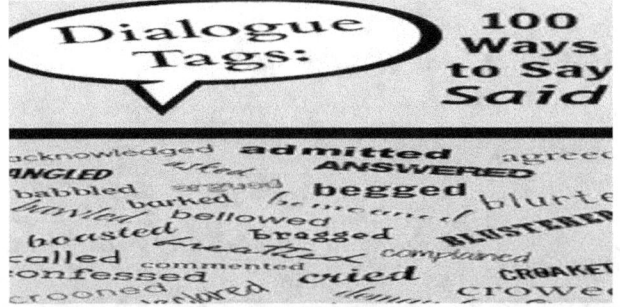

StumbleUpon: http://www.stumbleupon.com

Stumble Upon is a discovery engine that finds and recommends web content to its users. Its features allow users to discover and rate websites/videos etc.

Web pages, photos, and videos personalised to your own tastes

My Notes

Date Accessed
Where is it now?
Used For?
Comments

Twitter: https://twitter.com/

Twitter Tips for Beginners by Kevan Lee
http://blog.bufferapp.com/twitter-tips-for-beginners

Twitter Hacks by Neil Patel
http://blog.bufferapp.com/twitter-hacks

Advanced Twitter Tips by Kevan Lee
http://blog.bufferapp.com/advanced-twitter-tips

Twitter Feed for Abbey Johns

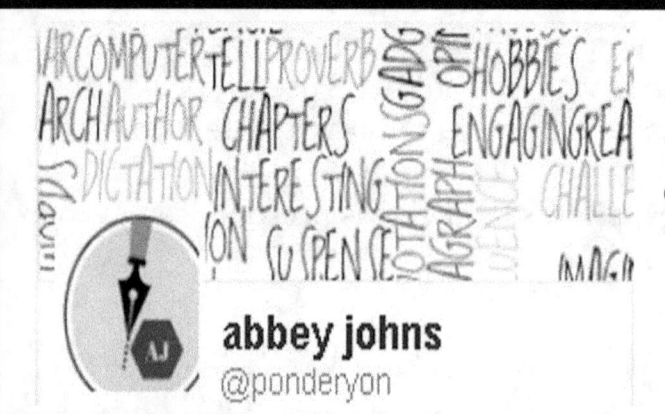

Follow me on Twitter!

abbey johns
@ponderyon

My Notes

Date Accessed
Where is it now?
Used For?
Comments

12. Work Quicker

Bogged down with writing and organising? Try these apps to make things go with a swing. Some great ideas to cut down work for Twitter and book production.

Alien Speech: Bit.ly/1Z9Gqyi

Alien Speech is a freeware Text to Speech program. Simply type in some text or load a text file, and Alien Speech reads it for you, at a speed and pitch of your choice.

Microphone Apps on Mobile Phones

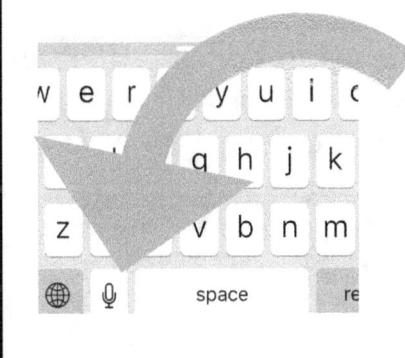

For Android, Microsoft and IOS - included
in smart phone keyboard as the norm.Use this for on-the- go notes or dictation straight into your blog or word processor.

My Notes

Date Accessed
Where is it now?
Used For?
Comments

Ringr: http://www.ringr.us

Connect with most people and countries on the planet, using Ringr for recording conversation.

Instantly download recording for editing and transcription. Available on Android, IOS, and PC. All you need is a person's email address.

Ideal for telephone interviews - then transcribe to a book.

Texter: Bit.ly/1YOm8tV

Windows only: this is a text substitution app. It saves you countless keystrokes by setting up a shortcut for common phrases you type, for example, I have set up my email address as ajpy; as soon as I type that combination of four letters and press enter, my email address magically appears in the text.

My Notes

Date Accessed
Where is it now?
Used For?
Comments

Typing Club: Bit.ly/1WCfskP

Master how to do touch-typing using this free game / educational program.

This online program assists learning and improving typing skills.

Practice can make perfect!

Voice Note: Bit.ly/1TdF7jn

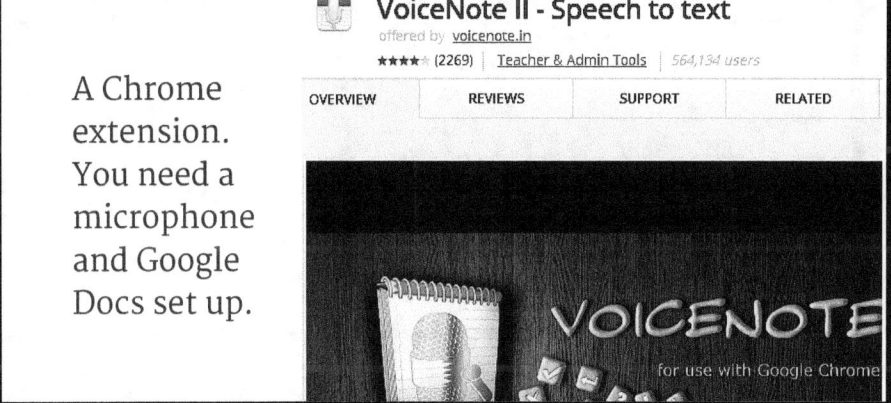

A Chrome extension. You need a microphone and Google Docs set up.

My Notes

Date Accessed
Where is it now?
Used For?
Comments

Winsplit Revolution: Bit.ly/1Z9HmCW

A small piece of coding that allows you to divide the screen up into 9 separate areas. Useful when working on lots of reference documents at once

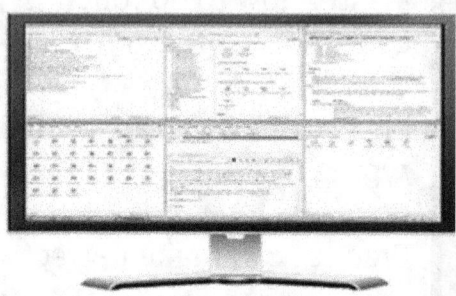

My Favourites:

Details:

My Notes

Date Accessed
Where is it now?
Used For?
Comments

13. Storage

Writers need lots of storage, whether on the go or in their favourite writing place. For me, this is at my PC. Here I have access to loads of files and collections of help and advice blogs and articles. The important part about storage though, is making sure you know where you have kept information, so it's easily retrievable.

Dropbox: https://www.dropbox.com

Dropbox is one of the safest and biggest cloud storage apps around.
You start with basic free account and add space by inviting friends or telling your friends on Facebook etc.
Upgrade to premium paid service for more capability.

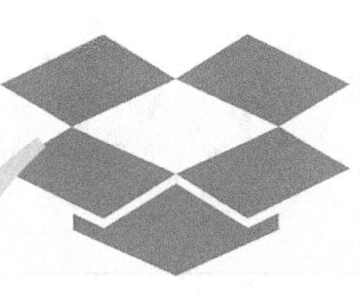

Evernote: https://evernote.com

Use Evernote on or offline. It is Dropbox's main competitor. I use Dropbox for my own documents, such as writing and books, and Evernote to store on line copies of PDF's, screenshots etc. In Evernote, I keep project to-do lists or just to jot down a reminder. Or, snap a picture of a sketch. Share with friends, family or work mates

My Notes

Date Accessed
Where is it now?
Used For?
Comments

Google Drive: https://www.google.com/drive

Get your files and photos from anywhere, on any device. With 15 GB free. Save any type of file.
Sign in with a free Google account.

iCloud: https://www.icloud.com

iCloud makes sure you always have the latest versions of your most important things — documents, photos, notes, contacts, and more — on all your devices.

My Notes

Date Accessed
Where is it now?
Used For?
Comments

Noteboard: https://www.noteboardapp.com

A great Chrome extension that allows you to save sticky notes and images. Available to use offline, with options for videos and colour coding.

OneDrive: https://onedrive.live.com/about/en-us

Get to your files and photos from anywhere, on any device.

Sign in with a free Microsoft account.

My Notes

Date Accessed
Where is it now?
Used For?
Comments

Pocket: https://getpocket.com

Pocket allows saving of articles or webpages you want to read later. Use on mobile, PC or Apple.

Pocket removes clutter from items and adjusts text settings for easier reading.

Zulu Pad: http://www.gersic.com/zulupad/

Zulu Pad is a notepad plus. Use it for class notes, appointments, to-do lists, favourite websites, annotated bookmarks, pretty much anything. Zulu Pad combines the best parts of a notepad with the best parts of a wiki. So if you type a name in Zulu it will become a link to a reference point. A concept made popular by Wikipedia.

Brilliant for researchers.

My Notes

Date Accessed
Where is it now?
Used For?
Comments

14. Writing Training Programmes

Try any of these writers programmes to enhance your
writing skills

Alison.com: Writing in English: Bit.ly/1qyxUgb

A free on-line language course for improving
your essay-writing abilities.

This course covers different styles of writing, including
comedy, descriptive, spy, thriller, instructional text,
opinion pieces, poetry, as well as punctuation. Also
there are guidelines to express yourself creatively in a
variety of writing styles.

MIT: Writing, Editing, and Publishing in Cyberspace:
Bit.ly/1qyxw1t

This is for writing prose
for public audiences –
specifically from a
personal
narrative perspective.
The focus is on
American popular
culture.

My Notes

Date Accessed
Where is it now?
Used For?
Comments

Open University: Write What You Know:
Bit.ly/1qwRt8S

Courses on writing for
beginners and more
advanced writers.

With a free eBook to
download as a starter.

Udemy: Secret Sauce of Great Writing: Bit.ly/1qwSCxc

Learn how to apply the key concepts of simplicity,
clarity, and elegance to your writing.

The course is aimed at professionals keen to upgrade
their writing skills to enhance their careers, or
businesses wishing to sharpen their corporate
documents.

With a free ebook to download.

My Notes

Date Accessed
Where is it now?
Used For?
Comments

Udemy: Write and Research with Research
Tools: Bit.ly/1qyxTsB

Here are all the tools and concepts for research, plus a
video tutorial about writing successful academic
proposals.
There are 720 various tools in the Research Tool box,
classified into 4 main categories: Literature-Review,
Writing a Paper, Targeting Suitable Journals, and
Enhancing Visibility and Impact Factor. Plus keyword
selection, citations, and references, mind mapping,
avoiding plagiarism and so on.

My Favourite:

Details:

My Notes

Date Accessed
Where is it now?
Used For?
Comments

15. Sales and Marketing

Content is important when writing, but if only your family read your prose then your book or blog is not going to become an international best seller or go viral. More work is needed after the writing to get your work out there and these apps and programmes can help.

PayPal: https://www.paypal.com

This is a worldwide on-line payments system that has replaced the traditional paper methods like cheques and money orders.

Set up your on-line store to sell digital products using PayPal. Accepts other credit cards also.

Good Reads: https://www.goodreads.com

Lets users track and rate books and network with other readers. Link this to your Amazon account to increase your public profile.

Gain access to a massive audience of more than 50 million book lovers. Goodreads is also a place to promote your books.

My Notes

Date Accessed
Where is it now?
Used For?
Comments

Logo Garden: http://www.logogarden.com

Create your logo design online for
your startup or small business
quickly & easily with the free DIY
logo generator

Amazon: http://www.amazon.com

Online retailer of books, movies,
music and games along with
electronics, toys, apparel, sports,
tools, groceries and general home
and garden items.

Search for top lists and keyword
research

My Notes

Date Accessed
Where is it now?
Used For?
Comments

Mailchimp: http://mailchimp.com

Online email marketing solution to manage subscribers, send emails, and track results.

Offers integration with other programmes and an easy to construct newsletter for subscribers.

Ebook Tracker:
http://tracker.kindlenationdaily.com

See the impact of marketing efforts and price changes on your book sales rank and pricing.

Know right away when sales start to flag on one of your titles, and see how your books rank and pricing data compare to those of your competitors.

My Notes

Date Accessed
Where is it now?
Used For?
Comments

YouTube Videos About Writing

Create your own channel for promoting your blog posts or books.
And learn writing skills. Try:

1. **Bit.ly/1TOVm1g: What makes a hero?**
2. **Bit.ly/1TOW4el: How to Build a Fictional World**
3. **Bit.ly/1TOWnGq: 3 Anti- Social Skills to Improve Writing**
4. **Bit.ly/1TOW0Mh: The Art of the Metaphor**

My Favourites

Details:

My Notes

Date Accessed
Where is it now?
Used For?
Comments

16. Communications

Keep in touch with collaborators, editors and customers wherever they are in the world.

Facebook Messenger:
https://www.messenger.com

Instant messaging as part of your Facebook account.
Use this for communicating with corroborators and
supporters.

Also has free video call capability now.

900 million people are on Messenger

Facetime: http://www.apple.com/mac/facetime

Apple's version of Skype - video conferencing for
groups of people or just one to one over the internet,
free of charge.

Can only use on Apple products though.

My Notes

Date Accessed
Where is it now?
Used For?
Comments

Google Hangout: https://hangouts.google.com

Use for video conferencing or one to one discussion over the internet. Useful when body language is important.

Message a friend or start a group conversation

Skype: https://www.skype.com

Hugely popular video conferencing and one to ones over the internet.

My Notes

Date Accessed
Where is it now?
Used For?
Comments

Survey Monkey: http://bit.ly/1PzIw59

SurveyMonkey is the world's most popular online survey software. It's easy to create polls and survey questionnaires for reader satisfaction and what your email list want you to blog about next.

My Favourites:

Details:

My Notes

Date Accessed
Where is it now?
Used For?
Comments

17. Gems and General

These apps and programmes don't really fit into a category type.
This section includes fun and quirky things to try, and some important apps that I couldn't do without.

Apache Open Office: Bit.ly/1TLpVEV

A free version of office
applications, just as good as
the real thing.
Mimics Word, Excel etc.
Great resource.

Calibre: https://calibre-ebook.com

An amazing computer programme for book writing. It
does just about everything; from conversions to E pub,
to keeping your eBooks in one place. See the HTML
behind the scenes for books, and how to change
coding.

Too much to say here, so have a look at the video:
https://youtu.be/6J1usDkKJKE

My Notes

Date Accessed
Where is it now?
Used For?
Comments

Count Down Timer: Bit.ly/1TLqTRJ

Run up to 40 countdown timers, with an audio alert and a popup window. You can also choose to run a program or open a URL in your default browser when the timer goes off.

Timers are set for days/hours/minutes/seconds, and restarts with the accurate remaining time when opened again.

Grimace Project: http://www.grimace-project.net

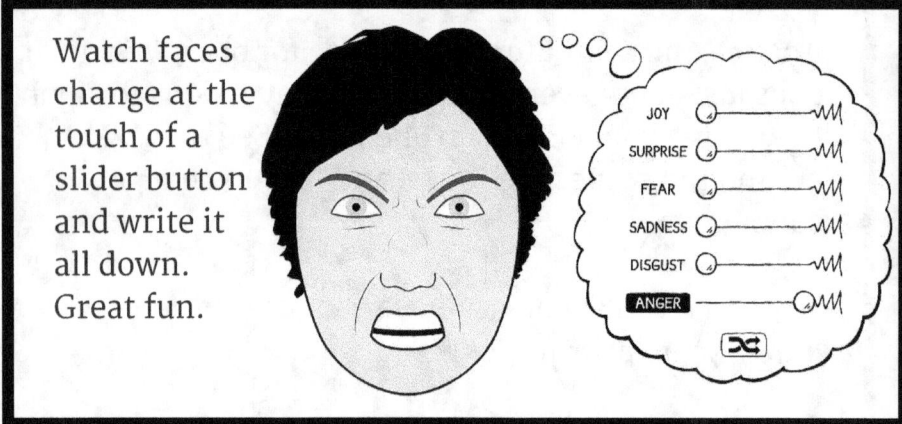

Watch faces change at the touch of a slider button and write it all down. Great fun.

My Notes

Date Accessed
Where is it now?
Used For?
Comments

Hanx Writer: Apple.co/1qyBirF

Makes an old-fashioned click clack of a typewriter as you type - quirky but great. Once it was the most popular app in the USA, launched by Tom Hanks. Confused?
A fun app rather than a practical one.

Watch the video here:
https://www.youtube.com/watch?v=Z3dvZSSqCj8

iPassword: Apple.co/1qyBaIz

I use this password manager for all apps with encryption, password protection, and backup.

For a comparison of password apps and features for 2016 go to: *http://bit.ly/28IAQ36*

My Notes

Date Accessed
Where is it now?
Used For?
Comments

Keyboard Shortcuts: Bit.ly/1YOmnp2

List of all the keyboard shortcuts you need for the major inputting keyboards and accessibility (from Wikipaedia).

Action	Windows	Mac OS	KDE / GNOME	Emacs	Vim
File menu	Alt + F , or F10 then F	Ctrl + F2 , then F (requires full keyboard access active, using System Preferences > Keyboard > Keyboard Shortcuts > Full Keyboard Access > All Controls. Alternatively use Ctrl + F7 to toggle this setting.)	Alt + F	Meta + `, then f	Alt + f (gvim) or Ctrl + e (vim + NERDTree)
Edit menu	Alt + E	Ctrl + F2 , then E	Alt + E	Meta + `, then e	Alt + e (gvim)

Merge PDF's: http://www.pdfmerge.com

This really simple utility allows you to join pdfs into one long document for workbooks, such as this one.

I used PDF Merge for putting this workbook together.

My Notes

Date Accessed
Where is it now?
Used For?
Comments

PDF Escape: http://www.pdfescape.com

Edit PDF's and fill in forms.

PktWriters App:apple.co/1qyAVoe

Do you enjoy reading stories? Do you enjoy writing stories? If so then Pocket Writer is for you.

Write your own content and get comments from other readers. Has a wonderful user-friendly screen.

My Notes

Date Accessed
Where is it now?
Used For?
Comments

Scribus: https://www.scribus.net

Open source desktop publishing with a user-friendly interface.

Scribus supports professional publishing features, such as newsletters, posters and PDF creation. Also unexpected touches, such as powerful vector drawing tools and support for a huge number of file types.

I've not tried it but it looks great.

Sway: https://sway.com

From Microsoft, it's the next step up from PowerPoint. Sway makes it quick and easy to create and share polished, interactive reports, presentations, personal stories, and more.

Have a look at one made by Microsoft: *https://sway.com/universe_cheatsheet*

Easy to use and produces a professional finish.

My Notes

Date Accessed
Where is it now?
Used For?
Comments

Trello: http://trello.com

Keep all your appointments and projects under control. Use your diary to set reminders and alerts. Share with team members.

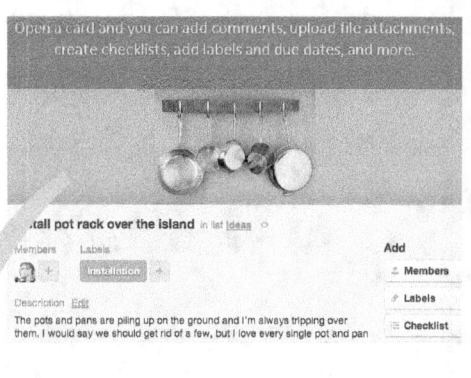

Word Count Tracker: Bit.ly/1qyB8jK

Paste your work into this online tool. A good tool if you want to check your word count and have no other means.

My Notes

Date Accessed
Where is it now?
Used For?
Comments

Word Meter: Bit.ly/1TLwSpC

Add the website to your workspace and hey-ho you have a tiny little counter to watch. See how many words you write in one session or set yourself a target word count.

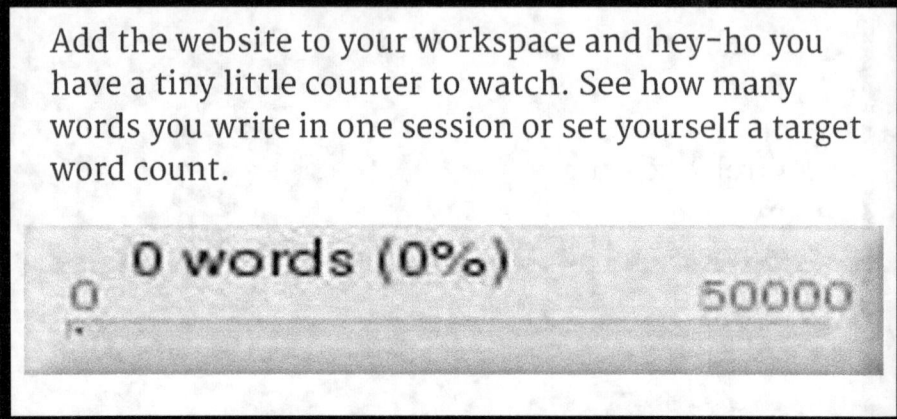

Your Sky: http://www.fourmilab.ch/yoursky

Enter latitude and longitude, date and time, to get a picture of the night sky for your book or historical novel

Aim Point	Right Ascension:	0h	
	Declination:	0°	● North ○ South
	Find object in catalogue		

Aim Virtual Telescope

My Notes

Date Accessed
Where is it now?
Used For?
Comments

18. Bonus

My Top Paid Apps

I use lots of free tools, but I also pay for necessary tools or programmes for writing.
You might want to consider paying for some of these.
Many have a free trial for you to test
for usefulness first.

Advanced Fiction Writing: Bit.ly/1YOk7xV

Try the Snowflake method for writing a novel or buy
the book to get you started. Works for me.

The first few steps look like this:

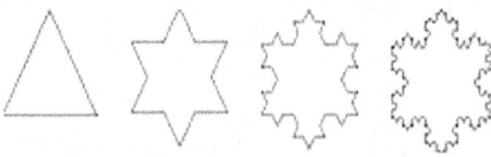

Dragon Naturally Speaking: Bit.ly/1TLy7oL

For voice to text capability – but you will have to train
your dragon before it performs accurately

Requires a system microphone.

My Notes

Date Accessed
Where is it now?
Used For?
Comments

Fiverr: https://www.fiverr.com

Go to this site and get work done (logos, short video's, infographics) for $5 or as it calls itself - the world's largest marketplace for services.

Technically a 'paid' service but for $5 it's almost free. You can also ask for extra services at a reasonable cost.

Hemingway: http://www.hemingwayapp.com

| B | I | :≡ | 1≡ | ◀≡ | ▶≡ | 🔗 | **P** | H1 | H2 | H3 |

Hemingway App makes your writing bold and clear.

The app highlights long, complex sentences and common errors; if you see a yellow sentence, shorten or split it.

For self-editing as you go. The programme highlights words and gives options. There is a readability scale of difficulty.

My Notes

Date Accessed
Where is it now?
Used For?
Comments

Rev recorder:
https://www.rev.com/voicerecorder

Dictate and send files for automatic transcription at $1 per minute.
Available for Android and IOS.

Used by many writers for the 'telephone interview with an expert' type of book.

Scrivener: https://www.literatureandlatte.com

For storyboarding and compiling long complex fiction and nonfiction writing. Most professionals claim to use this software. Complex to learn but excellent once you've mastered it.

My Notes

Date Accessed
Where is it now?
Used For?
Comments

TechSmith: https://www.techsmith.com

This software makes it easy to create engaging, polished screen images and videos you can share with anyone.

Snagit

Screen capture and so much more

Communicate with images and quick videos using Snagit's dynamic screen capture and editing tools.

Learn More Buy Now

Camtasia

Screen recording and video editing

Create professional-quality videos with Camtasia's powerful screen recording and video editing tools.

Learn More Buy Now

Relay

Organization-wide video creation and hosting

Roll out interactive videos across your organization with Relay's video creation and hosting system.

Learn More

My Favourites:

Details

My Notes

Date Accessed
Where is it now?
Used For?
Comments

19. Before You Go

I hope you find using The Writer's Toolkit
and Workbook helpful.

If you have enjoyed this toolkit for authors and writers,
I would really appreciate an honest review.

Maybe there are some other apps, hacks or videos, you
think should be included?
If so, please drop me an email at:
abbey.johns@ponder-yonder.com.

I'd love to hear from you

Or why not sign up to receive my newsletter
by going to my website:
Ponder Yonder.com

19. Glossary

PDF: Portable Document Format, is a universal file format developed by Adobe® that preserves all the fonts, formatting, graphics, and colour of a source document, regardless of who created it.

HTML: Hypertext Markup Language; just as the French speak French, so the web speaks in HTML. Learn this code if you want to write and/or design web pages. Or just tweak some website copy.

CSS: Cascading Style Sheets are used by web pages to help keep information in the proper display format. CSS files set up font, size, colour, spacing, border and location of HTML information on a web page, and used to create a consistent look throughout multiple pages of a website.

URL: Uniform Resource Locator. It is the address of a web page. Each page has its own unique web address (URL). My website URL is http://www.ponder-yonder.com.

RSS: Really Simple Syndication is a way of setting automatic content feeds from websites directly into your inbox rather than having to visit a site every day.

ePub: A specially formatted type of text document used as the source document for most books before publishing.

A/B Testing: Comparing the results of two types of marketing to see which one is more attractive to a buyer e.g. Red or White Roses, capital letters or script, and so on.

20. Alphabetical List of Resources

A

3D Book Cover http://bit.ly/1OzFFhn
Adobe Voice https://standout.adobe.com/voice
Advanced Fiction Writing (P) bit.ly/1YOk7xV
Alien Speech: http://www.aliensoftware.co.uk/index.asp
Alison bit.ly/1qyxUgb
Alltop http://alltop.com
Amazon http://www.amazon.com
Animoto https://animoto.com/
Apache Office https://www.openoffice.org/product/index.html
Apple Pages http://www.apple.com/ios/pages/
App Sumo http://www.appsumo.com
Apps Gone Free: https://itunes.apple.com/us/app/apps-gone-free-best-daily/id470693788?mt=8.

B

Beautiful Web Type http://hellohappy.org/beautiful-web-type
Bitley https://bitly.com/
Blog Topic: http://www.hubspot.com/blog-topic-generator
Blogger https://www.blogger.com
Blurb Booksmart http://www.blurb.com/make/booksmart
Bob Angus Ed Cal http://bit.ly/1PAsbNx
Buffer https://buffer.com/

C

Calibre https://calibre-ebook.com/
Canva https://www.canva.com/
Cold Turkey http://getcoldturkey.com/
Count Down Timer http://www.spacejock.com/yTimer.html
Cover Critics http://covercritics.com/
Create Space https://www.createspace.com/

Curator http://curator.co
CMI Ed Calendar:http://bit.ly/1PAssjw

D
DaFont http://www.dafont.com
Does My Cover Suck http://bit.ly/1YOntRw
Doodle http://doodle.com/
Dragon (P) http://www.nuance.com/dragon/index.htm
Dropbox https://www.dropbox.com/

E
Easy Book http://easybook-project.org/
Ebook tracker http://tracker.kindlenationdaily.com/
Editorial Calendars blog http://bit.ly/1PAqEHk
Evernote https://evernote.com/

F
Facebook Messenger https://www.messenger.com/
Facetime http://www.apple.com/mac/facetime/
Favicon http://www.favicon.cc/
Feedly https://feedly.com/
Fiverr (P) https://www.fiverr.com/
Flickr https://www.flickr.com/
FocusWriter http://gottcode.org/focuswriter/
FontFaceNinja http://www.fontface.ninja/
FontPark http://www.fontpark.net/en/
Font-to-Width http://www.fontpark.net/en/
Free Fonts http://www.1001freefonts.com/
Freepik http://www.freepik.com/about

G
Gimp https://www.gimp.org/
Gingko https://gingkoapp.com/

Go to Meeting http://www.gotomeeting.com/
Good Reads https://www.goodreads.co
Google Alerts: https://www.google.com/alerts
Google Analytics: https://analytics.google.com/
Google Docs: www.google.com/docs/about/
Google Drive: https://www.google.com/drive/
Google Earth: https://earth.google.com/
Google Fonts https://www.google.com/fonts
Google Hangouts: https://hangouts.google.com/
Grammerly: https://www.grammarly.com
Grimace Project: http://www.grimace-project.net

H
Hanx Writer http://apple.co/1qyBirF
Hemingway (P) http://www.hemingwayapp.com/
Hootsuite https://hootsuite.com/
Hubspot Ed Cal:http://bit.ly/1PArUKr

I
ibooks http://www.apple.com/ibooks/
Index Cards http://www.denvog.com/app/index-card/
Infogr.am https://infogr.am/
Instant Eyedropper http://instant-eyedropper.com/
iPassword http://apple.co/1qyBaIz

J
Jing http://jing.en.softonic.com/

K
Keyboard Shortcuts http://bit.ly/1YOmnp2
Kindle Scout https://kindlescout.amazon.com/

L
Lightbox Collaborative Ed Cal: http://bit.ly/1PAsoSn
Literary Terms http://writeworld.org/tagged/literary%20term
Logo Garden http://www.logogarden.com/

M
Mailchimp http://mailchimp.com/
Merge PDF's http://www.pdfmerge.com/
Microsoft Word https://office.live.com/start/Word.aspx
MIT training bit.ly/1qyxw1t

N
Neatorama bit.ly/1qyz1N7
Noisli http://www.noisli.com/
Noteboard https://www.noteboardapp.com/

O
One Page Spreadsheet http://bit.ly/1qyBFCq
OneDrive https://onedrive.live.com/about/en-us/
Open University bit./ly/1qwRt8S
Owl.ly http://ow.ly/

P
Pablo https://pablo.buffer.com/app
Password Apps Compare http://bit.ly/28IAQ36
Paypal https://www.paypal.com/
PDF Escape http://www.pdfescape.com/
Pinterest https://www.pinterest.com/
Pixaby https://pixabay.com/
PktWriter http://apple.co/1qyAV0e

Pocket https://getpocket.com/
Pomodoro Technique http://pomodorotechnique.com/
Postcron Ed Cal: http://bit.ly/1PArpAi
Powtoon https://www.powtoon.com/
PressThis https://wordpress.org/plugins/press-this/
ProWritingAid https://prowritingaid.com/

Q
Quora http://en.wikipedia.org/wiki/Quora

R
Recite This http://www.recitethis.com/
Rev recorder https://www.rev.com/voicerecorder
Ringr http://www.ringr.us/

S
Scribus https://www.scribus.net/
Scrivener (P) https://www.literatureandlatte.com/
Sigil http://sigil.en.softonic.com/
Simple Mind Maps http://www.simpleapps.eu/simplemind/
Size of Images bit.ly/1rQUtxV
Skype https://www.skype.com/
Soovle http://www.soovle.com/
Storybook http://www.novelist.ch/joomla/
Storystarter http://www.thestorystarter.com/
StumbleUpon http://www.stumbleupon.com/
Survey Monkey http://bit.ly/1PzIw59
Sway https://sway.com/

T
TechSmith (P) https://www.techsmith.com/
Texter bit.ly/1YOm8tV

Thesaurus http://www.thesaurus.com/
Title Generator http://www.noemata.net/pa/titlegen/
TypeGenius http://www.typegenius.com/
Typing Club bit.ly/1WCfskP

U
Udemy bit.ly/1qwSCxc
Udemy bit.ly/qyxTsb
Unsplash https://unsplash.com/

V
Vertical Measures Ed Cal:http://bit.ly/1PAsGHk
Voice Note bit.ly/1TdF7jn

W
Web.Search.Social http://bit.ly/1PAsqbj
What Font http://chengyinliu.com/whatfont.html
Wikipaedia https://www.wikipedia.org/
Winsplit http://winsplit-revolution.en.softonic.com/
Word Count Tracker http://bit.ly/1qyB8jK
Word Meter http://wordmeter.herokuapp.com/picometer
Word Web http://wordweb.info/free/
Wordcounter http://www.wordcounter.com/
Wordle http://www.wordle.net/
WordLists http://writeworld.org/tagged/word%20list
WordPress https://wordpress.com/
Wordpress Ed Cal: http://bit.ly/1PArUKy
World Building http://worldbuilding.stackexchange.com/
WP Clip Art http://www.wpclipart.com/index.html
Write or Die http://writeordie.com/
Writing for Kindle https://kdp.amazon.com

X
Xmind Map http://www.xmind.net/

Y
Your Sky http://www.fourmilab.ch/yoursky/
YouTube https://www.youtube.com/
Ywriter http://www.spacejock.com/yWriter5.html

Z
Zen Pen http://pen.io/zen/
Zulu Pad http://www.gersic.com/zulupad/

P = Paid App/Programme

21. My Notes

My Notes

My Notes

My Notes

My Notes

My Notes

My Notes

My Notes

My Notes

My Notes

My Notes

My Notes

My Notes

My Notes

My Notes

My Notes

My Notes

My Notes

My Notes

My Notes

My Notes

My Notes

My Notes

My Notes

My Notes

My Notes

My Notes

My Notes

My Notes

My Notes

My Notes

My Notes

My Notes

My Notes

My Notes

My Notes

My Notes

My Notes

My Notes

My Notes

My Notes

My Notes

My Notes

My Notes

My Notes

My Notes

My Notes

My Notes

www.ingramcontent.com/pod-product-compliance
Lightning Source LLC
Chambersburg PA
CBHW071349280526
45787CB00001B/267